The (Unofficial) UKIP Cookbook

British Food for British People

by

Marc Blakewill & James Harris

THE (UNOFFICIAL) UKIP COOKBOOK

Published by Blakewill & Harris

www.blakewillandharris.com

Printed and bound in the UK

ISBN: 978-0-9930978-0-5

About the authors

As well as writing for shows like *Horrible Histories*, *Russell Howard's Good News* and *The 4 O'Clock Club*, Marc Blakewill & James Harris have spent far too long over the years sitting together in cafés. It was in one of these godforsaken places, whilst chewing on a gristly sausage and wondering what on earth was in their scrambled egg, that they conceived The (Unofficial) UKIP Cookbook.

It is their first, and almost certainly last, cookbook.

Nigel Sewage, meanwhile, is a figment of his own imagination. He doesn't live in Kent.

This page is intentionally blank.

(Like the cheque we write to Brussels every year)

Contents

For my German wife and my Bulgarian cleaner, my Mozambiquan gardener, my Bangladeshi GP, my Latvian IT support guy, the Brazilian barista at my local café, the Nigerian carer who's looking after my aunt, my regular Somali mini-cab driver, my Irish accountant, my French editor and my Korean printer. I could've done it much better without you all.

Introduction

Congratulations on purchasing The (Unofficial) UKIP Cookbook. You are now in the vanguard of Britain's fight to retain its culinary independence. For far too long, this country has allowed itself to become swamped with foreign food and it's high time we sent it back to the kitchen with a resounding "Non!".

If we're prepared to protect our natural landscape or to save endangered species, why not endangered edibles such as the pork pie, jellied eels or marmite on toast?

The pretzel-munching, gazpacho-slurping metropolitan elite need to be taught a lesson. We will not sit idly by while our proud national heritage of eating pie and chips, fish and chips, and chips and gravy vanishes before our eyes. Henry V did not win at Agincourt so that we would eat snails. Churchill did not defeat the Nazis so that we would eat sauerkraut. And Thatcher did not swing her handbag in Brussels so that we would eat al dente pasta drizzled in extra virgin olive oil and freshly made pesto sauce.

Yes, it's time to raise the flag and repel the boarders.

Whether you care for Welsh rarebit, Scotch eggs, the full English breakfast or whatever they do in Northern Ireland, your country needs you.

Yours patriotically,

Nigel Sewage

Pointless EU Regulations to break whilst cooking: #1

After overcooking a roast, the kitchen will be a total bloody mess, so why not give it a good clean with a 1601 watt vacuum cleaner? Yes, a vacuum cleaner that is one whole unit of energy in excess of the absurd 1600 watt limit the EU has forced on house-proud British women against their will.

BARNSTORMING BRITISH
BREAKFASTS

Unapologetically uncontinental
offerings

|Croissant| Paltry pastry

INGREDIENTS

- EU-subsidised flour
- EU-subsidised eggs
- EU-subsidised milk
- Apart from that, mostly air

FOREIGNNESS

As foreign as a Parisian waiter with low self-esteem

Waking up to a French woman in the morning is one thing but waking up to a French breakfast is something else entirely. Nice curves and an air of haughtiness – that's fine in a lover but bloody useless on a plate. You want your morning meal to fortify you, not play hard to get.

THINGS TO WATCH OUT FOR

Cutting the croissant open in order to spread jam on it will result in its immediate disintegration. Just like France in 1940.

SEWAGE SAYS: **FLAKY FLIM FLAM**

|Full English| Patriotic artery-clogger

INGREDIENTS

- Bacon, eggs, sausages, tomatoes mushrooms, beans, toast. You know, proper food.

- Grease

PREPARATION

Fry the lot in a greasy pan until saturated in grease. Add grease to taste.

"Food to die for. Especially if you eat it every day."
- Sylvia Odolant, café-based paramedic

This magnificent meal contains all the major food groups: salt, fat and miscellaneous. For years it fuelled the valiant men and women who built the British Empire. As soon as we started eating cornflakes, we lost Rhodesia. So forget your cholesterol levels, say nuts to nutrients and do your patriotic duty. Eat stodge for Britain.

SERVING SUGGESTION

Best appreciated when troubled by the head pounding, dehydration and queasiness of a stonking hangover, i.e. Tuesday to Sunday.

SEWAGE SAYS: **THANK GOD IT'S FRY DAY**

|Muesli| You'd be nuts to eat it

INGREDIENTS

- Dust
- Things found down the back of the sof
- Moisture-sapping dryness

FOREIGNNESS

As foreign as an unclaimed rece in Brussels.

You can forgive the Swiss for their opaque banking system, and even their neutrality during the war but, Lord above, you cannot forgive them for the atrocity that is muesli. It's like eating pot pourri. There are only two occasions on which you can justifiably serve it as food. First, as a practical joke. Second, if you live on a farm and the pigs are starving.

THINGS TO WATCH OUT FOR

Muesli was apparently created by a Swiss doctor... Note to self: never get ill in Geneva.

SEWAGE SAYS: **BIRD FOOD FOR BIRD-BRAIN**

Porridge | Contains moral fibre

INGREDIENTS

- Rolled oats
- Water or milk
- Hardiness

PREPARATION

Pour water or milk on the oats and bring to the boil. Use a hob, not a microwave - it tastes better when you work for it.

The British Citizen test runs to several pages and asks questions about things like speed limits, Stonehenge and the length of Holly Willoughby's eyelashes. This tax-payer funded pub quiz is a complete waste of time and money. If you want to know if someone is genuinely British, you need ask only one question: "do you eat porridge?"

SERVING SUGGESTION

Add a small amount of salt or sugar to taste while pointing out obvious left-wing bias on Radio 4's the Today programme.

SEWAGE SAYS: **GO ON, GET YOUR OATS**

|Crêpe| Schrodinger's crêpe

INGREDIENTS

- Cardboard left out in the rain
- Butter left out of the fridge

FOREIGNNESS

As foreign as a windscreen wipe on a dodgem car.

It's just a pancake so why call it anything else? Not only that, but it can come in either sweet or savoury forms. Which is it, for heaven's sake?! This is supposed to be food, not an example of Heisenberg's Uncertainty Principle.

THINGS TO WATCH OUT FOR

The interior of the crêpe quickly becoming the exterior as the filling falls all over your shirt.

SEWAGE SAYS: **A LOAD OF OLD CRÊPE**

|Pancake| Properly named pan-made treat

INGREDIENTS

- Ebullient eggs
- Brave butter
- Fearless flour

PREPARATION

Mix in a bowl and pour into a pan while tapping out Land of Hope and Glory with a wooden spoon.

Dostoevsky said the test of civilisation is how you treat your prisoners. He was right – throw away the key. But the truest test is how you treat your meals. Giving them fancy names is just wrong. In Britain we call a pancake a pancake because it's a bloody pancake. We even eat pancakes on a day called Pancake Day. As transparent as our glorious legal system.

SERVING SUGGESTION

Toss in a frying pan while reflecting upon this nation's admirable love of home ownership.

SEWAGE SAYS: **PATRIOTICALLY PANTASTIC**

Pointless EU Regulations to break whilst cooking: #2

If forced into a situation where you have to prepare a salad, be sure to incorporate a cucumber of over 20cm in length that has a flex greater than 20mm, in direct and enjoyable contravention of European Commission Regulation no 1677/88.

LEGENDARY LOCAL
LUNCHES

No-nonsense nosh at noon

|Pizza| Unruly Italian hotchpotch

INGREDIENTS

- Not enough beef
- Not enough chees
- Too many anchovi

FOREIGNNESS

As foreign as
a dog on a lead
in Liverpool.

This greasy mess sums up everything that is wrong with Britain today: unnecessarily complicated, full of ingredients that don't mix and what's more, there is never enough pepperoni on a Spicy Hot One. It needs to be put back in its box and sent home. Come on, Britain. It's time to take away the pizza.

THINGS TO WATCH OUT FOR

 You'll probably be allocated a slice that's too small because other members round the table shout louder. Much like Brussels.

SEWAGE SAYS: **DELIVER IT BACK HOME**

|Ploughman's| Classic British mix

INGREDIENTS

- Doorsteps of bread
- Blocks of cheese
- Anything else that happens to be in or near the fridge

PREPARATION

Throw everything onto a wooden platter. Job done.

This is honest fare for hardworking British families. A brilliantly pragmatic collection of foodstuffs that doesn't fanny around with things like capers or anchovies. A big block of cheddar, that's what you want for a meal. A ploughman's doesn't set you up for the day, it sets you up for the week.

SERVING SUGGESTION

Best eaten with friends over a pint of real ale while discussing the scandalous size of the benefits bill.

EWAGE SAYS: **LUNCH FOR THE LIONHEARTED**

|Hamburger| Haplessly hamless

INGREDIENTS

- Horse
- Meerkat
- Whatever other animal happens to wander into the slaughterhouse

FOREIGNNESS

As foreign as a man on a bike that isn't dressed like a plonker.

For a nation as ludicrously litigious as the United States, it's odd that their only major contribution to international cuisine contravenes the Trades Descriptions Act. As anyone unfortunate enough to have eaten one knows, hamburgers don't contain ham. They also, very often, don't contain beef. They're an unappetising lawsuit in a bun.

THINGS TO WATCH OUT FOR

"Gourmet burgers" – a pathetic attempt to make eating a burger less shameful. Like calling a stripper a lapdancer.

SEWAGE SAYS: NO FUN IN A BUN

|Roast Beef| Albion's finest

INGREDIENTS

- Beef so fresh you can still hear the echo of a moo
- Roasted potatoes and veg
- Oodles of gravy

PREPARATION

Women cook it. Men carve it.

The Sunday roast is the pivot upon which the whole week turns, the pole around which all other meals revolve. It has everything an upstanding British family needs: nutrition, tradition and gravy. The EU can straighten our bananas, they can ban smoking within five miles of a child, but they can't take away our right to over-cooked meat.

SERVING SUGGESTION

Horseradish sauce adds tang to the meal, as does shaking your head in disgust at what the modern world has become.

EWAGE SAYS: **THE CHURCHILL OF LUNCHES**

|Sushi| A raw deal

INGREDIENTS

- Fish
- Not
- Cooked
- At
- All

FOREIGNNESS

As foreign as a vitamin in a Glaswegian's bloodstream.

Some British people claim to enjoy eating sushi but obviously they don't. They are simply trying to look cosmopolitan, to show other Guardian readers that they are a 'citizen of the world'. "Look at me!", they say. "I'm eating something that's just crawled out of the sea. How tolerant and forgiving of other cultures' stupidity am I?" A fool's errand.

THINGS TO WATCH OUT FOR

That feeling of uncertainty as to whether the cube you are forcing down is dolphin-friendly tuna or tuna-friendly dolphin.

SEWAGE SAYS: **ALL VERY FISHY**

|Kippers| No smoke without fish

INGREDIENTS

- Smoked herring
- Butter
- A pungent whiff

PREPARATION

Fry in a pan with butter until done. You know...cooked... edible. Which is what you're meant to do with food.

"A month's worth of salt in every mouthful. An incredible achievement."
- Seán Harte, gentleman nutritionist

For self-respecting UKIPPERs, kippers are one of the finest British foods known to humanity. Not only do you serve them cooked, they're smoked too. Yep, that's two lots of civilisation for the price of one. Get 'em down you.

SERVING SUGGESTION

Sure, you could have them for breakfast, but why not nip home at lunchtime and smoke up a pair of beauts before returning to work and stinking out your colleagues.

SEWAGE SAYS: **SMOKING HOT**

|Tacos | Best left on the shelf

INGREDIENTS

- Taco
- Stuff placed vaguely inside the taco, ready to spill all over you

FOREIGNNESS

As foreign as a fully-functioning queue in Italy.

There are many challenging world records: how many fat people you can fit in a phone box; how many claustrophobics you can fit in a Mini. Now there's another one, how many spoons of chilli you can fit in a taco. The current record? Three and a half. You could feed an army on this. If your army was a seven-year-old girl.

THINGS TO WATCH OUT FOR

Eat this with a knife and fork and you'll end up with a piece of taco shell lacerating your eye.

SEWAGE SAYS: **A WACKO WAY TO EAT**

|Cheese Sarnie| Bread of heaven

INGREDIENTS

- The finest cheese
- The finest pickle
- The finest butter
- Whatever bread comes to hand

PREPARATION

Butter one slice of bread. Add cheese THEN pickle. Cover with other slice.

"The cheese-and-pickle sandwich is unimprovable."
- Emma Taylor, never been abroad

Unlike the clam shell structure of the taco, the sandwich is constructed using free-standing slices of bread. You can therefore fit loads of stuff in like cheese and pickle. It's filling and flexible. Basically, tacos are a laughably small shack while the sandwich is a soaring monument to greatness.

SERVING SUGGESTION

Eat during typical British activity such as inventing the computer or conquering Everest.

EWAGE SAYS: **BEST THING SINCE SLICED BREAD**

|Chicken Madras| The spice of strife

INGREDIENTS

- Chicken
- Gunk that means you can't taste the chicken

FOREIGNNESS

As foreign as a black-and-white rainbow.

Chicken madras is nothing but a public health experiment served with naan. How much spice can you consume before you collapse head first into your pilau rice? This isn't food. This is come-and-have-a-go-if-you-think-you're-hard-enough.

THINGS TO WATCH OUT FOR

Turmeric. Whatever that is. The only place one should ever find turmeric is on a Scrabble board.

SEWAGE SAYS: **CURRY NO FAVOUR**

|Chip Butty| The king of food

INGREDIENTS

- Chips
- Bread
- Err, that's it

PREPARATION

Make it like you would a cheese and pickle sandwich but use chips instead.

Chips. Bread. On their own they are magnificent. Together they are truly unbeatable. What's more, the chip butty is an impromptu, do-it-yourself classic - just shove the chips into the bap and away you go. A cookbook could begin and end with the chip butty. As could your life.

SERVING SUGGESTION

Goes well with shouting politically incorrect abuse at a football match.

WAGE SAYS: **NO-NONSENSE NORTHERN NOSH**

Pointless EU Regulations to break whilst cooking: #3

After cooking your food, why not package and label it (even if you're just making it for yourself), ensuring that all potential allergens e.g. arsenic and uranium-235, are missing from the label. In this way, you will pleasingly flout EU Food Information Regulation No 1169/2011.

DOWNRIGHT DEPENDABLE

DINNERS

For hardworking British families

|Sweet & Sour Pork | No ebony and ivory

INGREDIENTS

- Sweet stuff
- Sour stuff
- Pork stuff

FOREIGNNESS

As foreign as an electric guitar solo on Songs of Praise.

We have four distinct tastes: sweetness, sourness, saltiness and bitterness. Oh, and "umami" - made up by the EU to create more red tape for small businesses. But here's the thing: they should all be SEPARATE. We don't put salt in our tea or lemon curd on our spuds. It's this contrary nonsense that is driving this country to the dogs. Which they also cook!

THINGS TO WATCH OUT FOR

 Your dish being referred to as a number. Saying: "I had a lovely 69 at my Chinese last night" might cause difficulties.

SEWAGE SAYS: **WORST OF BOTH WORLDS**

|Steak & Ale Pie| A great double-act

INGREDIENTS

- Steak
- Ale
- Pie

PREPARATION

Sample the ale first. Then get your missus to cook the damn thing while you get sloshed.

The history of Britain is the triumph of simplicity over complication, of practicality over pompousness, of sturdiness over showiness. It is the triumph of steak and ale pie. What other food builds muscle and gets you over the drink drive limit in such style?

SERVING SUGGESTION

Serve with fresh garden vegetables while reflecting on how this country invented both parliamentary democracy and darts.

SEWAGE SAYS: **ALL ALE THE PIE**

|Sea Food Paella| Gastro-crime

INGREDIENTS

- Illegal fish
- Illegal crustaceans
- Illegal cephalopod

FOREIGNNESS

As foreign as
a driver stopping
at a pedestrian
crossing in Madrid.

Despite the difficulties it entails, Britain abides by the Common Fisheries Policy. Well, there doesn't seem to be much evidence of that here. Any poor creature unfortunate enough to lurk in the Mediterranean seems to be in this ludicrous Noah's Ark of a dish. Sea food paella shouldn't be eaten, it should be prosecuted.

THINGS TO WATCH OUT FOR

65% of sea food paella is unpronounceable. 85% is inedible. 100% is wrong.

SEWAGE SAYS: **THEFT ON THE HIGH SEAS**

|Fish And Chips| Catch of the day

INGREDIENTS

- Cod or haddock that escaped the Norwegian nets

- King Edward tats

PREPARATION

Stand to attention whilst slicing the King Edwards, then fry the fish whilst sticking two fingers up at the Norwegians.

"My local chippie not only knows my name, he knows my cholesterol levels. That's called 'service'" - **Alan Fox, committed wearer of Union Jack pants**

Just like this proud island nation, fish and chips is the perfect marriage of land and sea. It's also full of saturated fat. The Nanny State and the BBC say that's bad for your health. Stuff them. If one is to die of a diet-related heart attack, it should be a heart attack made in Britain.

SERVING SUGGESTION

Wrap in yesterday's newspaper so you can be scandalised by the latest immigration figures on the way home from the chippie.

SEWAGE SAYS: **IT'S BETTER IN BATTER**

|Goat Curry| Seriously? How could you?

INGREDIENTS

- Freedom-loving ungulate

- Spices and sauce to cover the crime

FOREIGNNESS

As foreign as a High Court judge in a DIY store.

Some animals are there to be reared, slaughtered, chopped up and cooked, while others are there to look nice. Foreign people, hear this: the proper place for a Billy Goat is grazing in a field not simmering on a hob. If you're unsure, remember this rule: if you can take it to your vet, don't serve it with courgette.

THINGS TO WATCH OUT FOR

Having to say: "Waiter, waiter! There's a goat in my curry." No one will believe you. They'll just laugh.

SEWAGE SAYS: **THIS GETS OUR GOAT**

|Shepherd's Pie| This dish isn't sheepish

INGREDIENTS

- Minced lamb
- Mashed potato
- Vegetables
- Heartiness

PREPARATION

Cover the cooked mince and veg with mash and bake whilst blaming bad weather on gays.

If there's anything better than watching a lamb gambol in a field in our green and pleasant land then it's shoving one in an ovenproof dish and eating it. Lamb is so nutritious and tasty you'd almost think it was a vegetable. In fact, if it wasn't for the bureaucrats in Brussels, it probably would be.

SERVING SUGGESTION

Serve to guests as a hearty winter meal whilst assuring them that the dish contains no black sheep.

SEWAGE SAYS: **NO WOOLLY THINKING HERE**

|Chilli Con Carne| A calamity

INGREDIENTS

- Peppers
- Paprika
- Paint stripper

FOREIGNNESS

As foreign as Vladimir Putin caught reading a self-help book.

Alexander Fleming discovered penicillin when some mould accidentally fell into his petri dish. It has since saved many millions of lives. The Mexicans discovered chilli con carne when the contents of a spice rack fell onto a beef dish. It has since killed millions of taste buds.

THINGS TO WATCH OUT FOR

Eating this might invalidate your life insurance. But don't worry, the Nanny State will come to your rescue.

SEWAGE SAYS: CHILLI CON CARNAGE

|Beans On Toast| Bean feast

INGREDIENTS

- Baked beans
- Buttered toast
- Magnificent simplicity

PREPARATION

Heat the beans on the hob using traditional British electricity then pour onto toast.

"A man who is bored of beans on toast is bored of life."
- **Austin Sawyer, proud caravan owner**

Britons eat more baked beans per capita than any other nation on earth. And that's how it should be. The only thing nobler than a baked bean is a baked bean swimming in tomato sauce atop a slice of buttered toast. But careful with that bread! The crust must not be cut off. We must protect our borders.

SERVING SUGGESTION

Best eaten whilst throwing copies of the deplorable Human Rights Act on the fire.

SEWAGE SAYS: **WORKING MAN'S WONDER**

|Doner Kebab | Pitta it won't hold together

INGREDIENTS

- Stupidly thin bread
- Meat containing DNA of no known animal

FOREIGNNESS

As foreign as a road safety campaigner with a sense of humour.

The doner kebab is symptomatic of Europe's drastic manufacturing decline. It has dodgy raw materials, is constructed in no apparent order and falls apart quicker than a Fiat Uno left out in the rain. "Would you like chilli sauce with that, boss?" "No, thanks. I like my shoes the colour they are."

THINGS TO WATCH OUT FOR

Wondering why your stomach's become an impromptu research centre for botulism.

SEWAGE SAYS: **DONER DO IT**

|Cornish Pasty | This is no pastiche

INGREDIENTS

- Beef
- Potato
- Edible handles

PREPARATION

Ensure that your oven is British-made so that it is worthy of housing such a homegrown beast.

Foreign chefs are obsessed with concepts like "taste" and "flavour". It's all about "enjoying food". Nonsense. The most important thing food should have is structural integrity. And that's where Cornish pasties come in. They're so solid you could build a house out of them. Or a pub. Which is another thing foreigners don't understand.

SERVING SUGGESTION

Eat outside a factory in the Midlands while complaining that Mini Coopers are now basically German cars.

SEWAGE SAYS: **THE PRIDE OF CORNWALL**

Pointless EU Regulations to break whilst cooking: #4

Once you've cooked your marvellous nosh, make a totally spurious claim for its health benefits in contravention of European Commission Regulation no 1924/2006. Examples include: roast beef improves your hand-eye co-ordination; custard can give you eternal life; pork pies help you fly.

CLEARLY COMMONSENSE
COMESTIBLES

The snack of firm leadership

|Prawn Crackers| Prawn fraud

INGREDIENTS

- No prawns
- Still no prawns
- Where the hell are the prawns?!

FOREIGNNESS

As foreign as a jalapeno in a Geordie's kebab.

First question: where's the prawn? Nowhere, that's where. These crackers are basically homeopathic food. No prawn, just the memory of prawn. If you left some Styrofoam overnight on Brighton pier, you'd create a finer sea-food snack than this. File under "total and utter disgrace".

THINGS TO WATCH OUT FOR

Having to eat these on a drip to prevent salt-induced dehydration.

SEWAGE SAYS: **YOU MUST BE CRACKERS**

|Pork Scratchings| Superlative snack

INGREDIENTS

- Not sure to be honest but there is probably pig's eyebrow in there somewhere

PREPARATION

Can only be bought in pubs with fruit machines and wall-to-wall carpets.

In this age of obsessive, neo-narcissistic health concerns, pork scratchings have become the pariahs of pub snacks. Eat these and you'll be accused of attempted suicide. But pork scratchings have helped make Britain what it is today. A country full of people who should live a lot longer than we do.

SERVING SUGGESTION

To be washed down with a port and brandy while arguing British police officers should not be able to speak a foreign language.

SEWAGE SAYS: **PUTS HAIRS ON YOUR CHEST**

|Poppadoms| Oversized crisps

INGREDIENTS

- Oversized flour
- Oversized vegetable oil

FOREIGNNESS

As foreign as a Media Studies graduate building something useful like a bridge.

Poppadoms are, let's face it, big crisps. And crisps should come ready-broken in packets. Having to break them up yourself is just a load of bureaucratic nonsense. And then they expect you to dip them in things! Ridiculous! The poppadom must learn its true place in the hierarchy of wafer-thin fried carbohydrates. Bottom of the pile.

THINGS TO WATCH OUT FOR

You'd assume they come in different flavours like proper crisps. But no. Nothing. Not even cheese & onion. Just bland nonsense. Appalling.

SEWAGE SAYS: **POP THEM ON A PLANE**

|Crisps| Proper-sized crisps

INGREDIENTS

- Potatoes
- Oil
- Salt
- FLAVOURS!

PREPARATION

Don't bother.
Available from all
good crisp outlets.

"Prawn cocktail followed by beef and tomato finished off with cheese and onion.
A great British three-course meal." - **Louisa Gummer, right-thinking person**

Practical and character-building, the humble potato crisp is at the heart of our national life. Imagine a childhood without licking the salt and vinegar flavour off your fingers. Impossible. So, go on. Give your child the gift of cherished memories. Give them salt-induced hypertension. Give them crisps.

SERVING SUGGESTION

Best eaten in the pub accompanying a decent British ale while discussing why the country is going to the dogs.

SEWAGE SAYS: **CRISPY GOODNESS**

|Olives| Why would you bother?

INGREDIENTS

- Fruit of the olive tree grown to provide shade for lazy farmers

FOREIGNNESS

As foreign as a spinal column in a LibDem MP.

If anything can explain why the European Union is doomed, it's the olive. Guests are offered a bowl of them and invited to take a couple. But they're so small everyone keeps coming back for more, dipping their fingers into the magic communal bowl. Until, of course, the olives run out and everyone blames the Germans.

THINGS TO WATCH OUT FOR

Like the voice of a BBC continuity announcer, the olive is only the prelude to something even more disappointing.

SEWAGE SAYS: **A POOR MAN'S PLUM**

|Stuff On A Stick |

You won't
feel a prick

INGREDIENTS

- Cheese and pineapple
- Pickled onions
- Mini sausages
- Basically, anything that will go on a stick!

PREPARATION

Put the stuff on sticks. Sorted.

"No buffet is complete until you've lacerated your tongue with a cocktail stick."
- **Chris Orrow, hardened party-goer**

You know what you're getting with cheese and pineapple on a stick. You're getting cheese and pineapple on a stick. Same goes for your pickled onion and your cocktail sausage. Basically, you get out what you put in. Which is more than can be said of the UK benefits system.

SERVING SUGGESTION

With cheese, attach a little Union Jack to each stick to make it absolutely clear this is commonsense British fare - none of this pretentious "runny" foreign nonsense.

SEWAGE SAYS: **HIT ON A STICK**

|Mayonnaise| French fancy

INGREDIENTS

- White gloop
- White gunk
- Vinegar

FOREIGNNESS

As foreign as bead curtains in a nuclear fallout shelter.

It is no accident that the moral decline of Britain has coincided with the rise of mayonnaise. A dressing should pair itself with a dish and live monogamously ever after. Not mayonnaise. It flaunts itself as a dressing for all occasions. "Come here," she whispers, "and I shall spread myself for you – anytime, anywhere, on anything". Beware this floozy!

THINGS TO WATCH OUT FOR

 Eating it and expecting to enjoy it, particularly once a splodge of the blasted stuff has dripped down your front and into your lap.

SEWAGE SAYS: **PROMISCUITY IN A JAR**

|Gravy| The lifeblood of Britain

INGREDIENTS

- Beef stock
- Okay, chicken or lamb stock if you must
- Definitely not vegetable or onion stock

PREPARATION

Pour hot water on the stock and stir.

Gravy is a fine and faithful sauce. It's poured on meat, veg and potatoes and that's it. When you reach for that stock cube, you know what to expect of gravy and gravy knows what to expect of you.

SERVING SUGGESTION

Ladle onto roast beef and Yorkshire pudding as a tear of patriotic pride rolls down your cheek.

SEWAGE SAYS: **A SAUCE OF HOPE**

|Hummus| A heap of halitosis

INGREDIENTS

- Suspicious brown stuff
- Little bits of who-knows-what

FOREIGNNESS

As foreign as a chastity belt in Magaluf.

If the spirit of the EU could be rendered in food, it would be hummus. Ingredients that can get on jolly well on their own, together become a useless splodge of blandness. If the chickpea can be liberated from this homogenous mush then so can we.

THINGS TO WATCH OUT FOR

Friends assuming that you are seriously ill as you don't appear to be eating solids.

SEWAGE SAYS: **SHORT FOR HURLSOME MUS**

|Brown Sauce| Ooh, you are saucy

INGREDIENTS

- Tomatoes, molasses, dates, tamarind, spices, vinegar and raisins. Sounds odd but it works.

PREPARATION

You're busy. You've got stuff to do. Don't bother making it. Get it from the shops.

This spicy delight isn't a condiment, it's a genuine snack. Eat it with chips and you know the chip is simply a brown sauce delivery system. If you could only take three items with you to a desert island, it should be The Complete Works of Jeremy Clarkson, a Union Jack and a bottle of HP.

SERVING SUGGESTION

Can be eaten on its own but also goes well with other British food such as chips, chip butties and over-cooked roast beef.

SEWAGE SAYS: **ONCE YOU'VE HAD BROWN...**

|Guacamole| Unholy moly

INGREDIENTS

- Lime
- Chilli
- Avacado
- Stuff that shouldn't get past customs

FOREIGNNESS

As foreign as a Marxist at Last Night Of The Proms

These days, the fashion for trying new things has got completely out of hand. Why else would anyone want to eat this day-glo muck? We must stick to what we know and what we know works best. In Britain, avocado is, and will always be, the colour of your bathroom suite.

THINGS TO WATCH OUT FOR

The Aztecs ate this stuff. Do you want to eat the food of a failed civilisation?

SEWAGE SAYS: **GREEN, UNPLEASANT, BLAND**

|Mushy Peas| Peas peas me

INGREDIENTS

- Lots of sugar
- Lots of salt
- Add peas to taste

PREPARATION

Soak the peas overnight with baking soda while you get soaked with gin.

"So wonderfully, radioactively green, you could eat this in the dark"
- **Angela Fox, mushy peas-survivor**

Okra, yam, cassava, papaya. No, they're not recent winners of the Prize for Overseas Fiction, they're fruit and veg that might end up on your plate in today's happy-clappy liberal Britain. It's political correctness gone bonkers. What this country needs is British veg for hardworking British people. What this country needs is peas. Mushed up a bit. Mushy peas.

SERVING SUGGESTION

Eat with chunky chips in the depths of winter while wearing a northern football shirt. Like fans of Newcastle Utd. Or that other northern city.

SEWAGE SAYS: **GIVE PEAS A CHANCE**

|Taramasalata| Pink slime

INGREDIENTS

- Lemon juice and milk!
- Olive oil and fish eggs!
- No, really!

FOREIGNNESS

As foreign as a condom machine in a convent.

Is there anything more hilarious than a dip made from fish eggs? Yes, at some point in history some foreigner saw a fresh cod and thought: "Hey. We can remove the roe, mix it with lemon juice, milk and olive oil and call it food." You can't make this stuff up. We gave the world the Industrial Revolution. They gave us indigestion.

THINGS TO WATCH OUT FOR

Whatever you do, for God's sake don't let your kids mistake it for Angel Delight. The poor sods will have nightmares for a week.

SEWAGE SAYS: **DON'T DIP INTO THIS**

|Scotch Egg| Hard-boiled hero

INGREDIENTS

- Egg
- The outside stuff that goes round the egg

PREPARATION

Cover the egg in the outside stuff until it's perfectly spherical. Marvel at the roundness of it all.

"If there's a finer spherical egg-based snack on the planet, I'm yet to sample it."
- Fiona Underhill, picky bed and breakfast owner

When a chicken lays an egg it has two devout wishes. First, that it grows up to be a proud British chicken like its mother. Second, that it becomes a Scotch egg. No other country could produce this snack. No other country could eat this snack. No other country would even consider this snack. Be proud.

SERVING SUGGESTION

Purchase from a poorly refrigerated unit in a motorway service station then eat while driving at 77mph singing along to Top Gear's Great Driving Power Ballads Volume IV.

SEWAGE SAYS: **AS SURE AS EGGS IS EGGS**

How to deny man-made climate change while cooking: #1

Take the temperature of the outside air with a British-made thermometer. Cook a meal with the oven on full. After the meal is ready open your kitchen windows to let the heat out. Wait a few seconds then take the temperature of the air outside. Any difference? Of course not. Man-made climate change is codswallop.

STAUNCHLY SIMPLE

STARTERS

Not a Maastricht morsel in sight

| Borscht | Disgrace from behind the Iron Curtain

INGREDIENTS

- Probably some sort of ritual animal blood
- Radioactive water from Chernobyl

FOREIGNNESS

As foreign as eating outdoors

This beetroot-based soup is popular in Ukraine, Belarus, Poland, Estonia, Lithuania, Latvia, blah, blah, blah. If it was entered into the Eurovision song contest it would win by a mile. And what would an unpretentious British soup get? That's right. Nul points. Borscht is a liquid symbol of all that is wrong with Europe. It's time to fight back. It's time to slurp British!

THINGS TO WATCH OUT FOR

If you spill some, it'll leave a horrible red stain - just like the Warsaw Pact. And it'll take just as long to wash away.

SEWAGE SAYS: **SIMPLY THE WORSCHT**

|Beetroot Soup|

Delight from this Sceptred Isle

INGREDIENTS

- British beetroot
- British water
- British salt
- British pepper

PREPARATION

Bring to the boil whilst humming Jerusalem.

"Borscht? You can't trust any dish that has 5 consonants in a row. It's plain common sense." - **Daniel Gosling, a bloke down the pub**

When they start serving borscht at your local golf club you know you're in trouble. It is unbridled immigration in a bowl. Ensure the integrity of our nation's borders by insisting upon good, solid, hearty, British beetroot soup instead. How to tell if you're supping on beetroot soup and not some foreign muck? Ask yourself: "Are you in Britain?" If "yes", then yes. Sorted.

SERVING SUGGESTION

Best enjoyed while bemoaning the number of bilingual people in Britain.

SEWAGE SAYS: IMPOSSIBLE TO BEET

|Pickled Herring| A bit of a pickle

INGREDIENTS

- Socialist fish
- Left-wing vinegar

FOREIGNNESS

As foreign as an amusing politically correct comedian.

With their generous benefits, good child care and love of the environment, you might think Scandinavia is a socialist utopia. That's until you look at what they have to eat: pickled fish. That's right, folks - they've spent so much money on bio-degradable ABBA CDs and carbon-neutral vibrators they can't afford to cook their own food.

THINGS TO WATCH OUT FOR

Every time you eat this stuff, you're just encouraging social democracy.

SEWAGE SAYS: **FEED IT TO THE CAT**

|Jellied Eels| East End elegance

INGREDIENTS

- Eels
- Some sort of jelly to put the eels in

PREPARATION

Kill the eel, chop it up, boil it, allow it to cool. Sorted, guv'nor.

We British are excellent at putting food in jars: strawberry jam, raspberry jam and jellied eels. Name something of worth that foreigners have put in a jar? Einstein's brain. Yeah. Try eating that. Jellied eels don't seem so bad now, do they?

SERVING SUGGESTION

Best enjoyed while flouting the EU Working Time directive.

SEWAGE SAYS: **THE REEL DEEL**

|Bruschetta| Random stuff on bread

INGREDIENTS

- Stuff from the back of the cupboard
- Stuff stuck to the back of the fridge

FOREIGNNESS

As foreign as a poetry reading in a motorway service station.

Onion, tomato, balsamic vinegar, basil, olive oil. No, that's not the contents of a salad, it's what the Italians think is acceptable to put on bread. If you can call a baguette bread. Honestly. You'd have to be high on illegal drugs to come up with such a ludicrous concoction and you'd have to be even higher on even more illegal drugs to eat it.

THINGS TO WATCH OUT FOR

Whatever you do, for heaven's sake don't pronounce it correctly. Do you want to be mistaken for a Liberal Democrat MEP?

SEWAGE SAYS: **WILL MAKE YOU BRUSQUE**

|Bread & Dripping| Fat on toast. And why not.

INGREDIENTS

- Animal fat
- Bread
- A knife and a plate to reassure you that it is food

PREPARATION

Place a slab of fat on the bread. Eat it. Enjoy it.

"Tastes just as good as it sounds."
- John Gowers, a man you want on your side in a fight

They say coal and iron was the fuel of the Industrial Revolution. Poppycock. It was bread and dripping. Generations of northerners not only survived on this stuff, they ate it for fun. Vitamins, fibre, anti-oxidants. You won't find any of that nonsense here. Bread and dripping is for men.

SERVING SUGGESTION

Turn the lights off, crouch under the kitchen table and imagine you're eating it down a coal mine.

SEWAGE SAYS: **MAY THE LARD SAVE US**

|Sauerkraut| Sour shredded cabbage - ugh

INGREDIENTS

- Shredded cabbage
- Lactic acid and bacteria. That's right. Bacteria. On purpose

FOREIGNNESS

As foreign as a trampoline in an old people's home.

Let's be clear. Pickled cabbage must not get a foothold in our national diet. Before we know it, we will be ending our sentences with verbs and developing a highly efficient value-added manufacturing sector. That's just not British. We will fight it in Tesco's; we will fight it in Waitrose; to sour cabbage, we will never surrender.

THINGS TO WATCH OUT FOR

 Jars of this outrage are taking up valuable shelf space that could be devoted to more patriotic foods like jellied eels and marmite.

SEWAGE SAYS: **NEIN, FRITZ!**

|Cabbage Soup|

Cabbage broth. Yum.

INGREDIENTS

- Cabbage, water, salt and pepper. You'd think there'd be more to it, but not so

PREPARATION

Boil the cabbage in the water until it becomes soup-like.

Nothing says "Britain" better than good old cabbage soup. It's a classic hot meal, it's devastatingly nutritious and if you hold your nose while you eat it, you'll even think it tastes good. Brilliant for curing colds and lowering culinary expectations.

SERVING SUGGESTION

Best eaten at the dinner table while discussing how the Euro is simply a new form of German imperialism.

WAGE SAYS: **CABBAGE WITHOUT THE BAGGAGE**

|Garlic Bread| For vampire hunters only

INGREDIENTS

- Self-regarding bread
- Smug garlic

FOREIGNNESS

As foreign as a Human Rights lawyer that you don't want to punch in the face.

You might think this is a harmless snack or starter, but if you do, you'd be dead wrong. Garlic bread is an outrider of EU totalitarianism. If we continue to accept this as part of our national diet, they know we will accept anything. First garlic bread then electric cars, and before you know it, Angela Bloody Merkel telling you how to wipe your backside.

THINGS TO WATCH OUT FOR

Restaurants trying to dupe you into thinking this is acceptable as a starter.

SEWAGE SAYS: **A STINKER**

|Marmite On Toast| Toasty

INGREDIENTS

- Sovereign bread
- Independent butter
- Free marmite

PREPARATION

Spread the marmite on the toast with a stainless knife forged in the steelworks of Sheffield.

Yeast is responsible for three of the greatest things known to mankind: beer, bread and marmite. You could live on nothing else for a month and still be able to swim the English Channel in your Union Jack underpants. Yeast might be a eukaryotic microorganism but there's no EU about it at all. This fine, freedom-loving fungus is British through and through.

SERVING SUGGESTION

Throw the toast in the air. It will land marmite-side up. Unlike top-heavy state-subsidised foreign toast.

SEWAGE SAYS: **A FEAST OF YEAST**

How to deny man-made climate change while cooking: #2

Hold a barbecue in your greenhouse. Witness how the greenhouse fills up with smoke. Also notice all the lefties queuing up outside ready to say "I told you so". But then open the greenhouse door to allow the smoke to disperse. The greenhouse is now habitable again, and the conclusion is obvious: greenhouse gas emissions should actually be increased. Witness the lefties scuttling off with their tails between their legs at that little scientific bombshell.

MAJESTIC MONOCULTURAL
MAINS

No offshore offal on offer here

|Wiener Schnitzel| Austrian abomination

INGREDIENTS

- Lifeless calf
- Pointless breadcrumbs
- Silly name

FOREIGNNESS

As foreign as a tomato in a fruit salad.

It's hard to write about wiener schnitzel without contravening the UK Race Relations Act 1976. Meat in breadcrumbs? That's not just wrong, it's immoral. Thankfully this frightful dish has yet to become as established in the national diet as other invasive species. We cannot rest on our laurels though. These Teutons do have ways of making us eat.

THINGS TO WATCH OUT FOR

When the chef's "recommendation" becomes the chef saying "you will have this or else", you know it's going to be wiener schnitzel.

SEWAGE SAYS: **YOU DIED IN VAIN, YOUNG CA**

|Veal Pie| British Pre-Beef Beauty

INGREDIENTS

- Meat of a young calf (best not to think about it)
- Pastry

PREPARATION

Place the veal in the pastry and cook in an oven until it becomes a pie.

There is surely nothing more British than a pie. Solid and dependable. Filling not flashy. Forget free education or high-speed broadband, every British child should have unfettered access to over-cooked, inhumanely reared animal in pastry. It's the bedrock of our proud island nation.

SERVING SUGGESTION

Eat while cultivating a dashed fine moustache and watching re-runs of the Dambusters.

WAGE SAYS: **PROPER DISH FOR PROPER CATTLE**

|Goulash| Flash name for plain food

INGREDIENTS

- Foreign steak
- Foreign onions
- Paprika (all paprika is foreign)

FOREIGNNESS

As foreign as a Viking at a peace conference

Goulash is basically stew. But because it's got a fancy-sounding foreign name, the metropolitan liberal elite think it's superior to our own meat-based casseroles. You don't travel to work on a vonat, do you? Or sit on a szék? No. Because they're Hungarian words and this isn't Hungary. Yet. So, come on. Let's re-assert ourselves. Let's call a spade a spade. Let's call a stew a stew.

THINGS TO WATCH OUT FOR

Being invited to eat this at the Gay Hussar. So many shades of wrong.

SEWAGE SAYS: I'D RATHER GO HUNGARY

|Stew| Meat. Potatoes. Bosh.

INGREDIENTS

- Potatoes
- Meat
- Carrots
- Simplicity

PREPARATION

Chop it all up and shove it in the oven before going for a frame of snooker.

The unapologetically British word "stew" is both a noun and a verb: you can eat stew and you can stew meat. Not that anyone under the age of 50 would know the bleeding difference. New-fangled leftie teaching methods must be dropped in favour of teaching kids grammar. Ideally with the threat of low-level violence. Ideally after a plate of stew.

SERVING SUGGESTION

To be savoured while sticking pins into a life-size doll of the leader of the National Union of Teachers.

SEWAGE SAYS: **STEW-PENDOUS**

|Moules Marinières | Never mind the molluscs

INGREDIENTS

- Moules - that's mussels to you and me

- Marinières – nope, not a clue

FOREIGNNESS

As foreign as a cyclist waiting patiently at a red traffic light.

If you've never had mussels in white wine and garlic, count yourself lucky. It's a 90:10 meal. 90% of the time is spent trying to eat the last 10% of it. Just when you think you've found the last mussel, another appears from under some now completely stone-cold fries. A plate is where a meal should take place, not the venue for a game of mollusc hide and seek.

THINGS TO WATCH OUT FOR

Expending more calories hunting down and opening the shells than you gain from eating their meagre garlic-soaked contents.

SEWAGE SAYS: COMPLETE FAFF

|Fish Fingers| Nothing fishy about these

INGREDIENTS

- Fish in a finger
- Breadcrumbs

PREPARATION

Buy from any self-respecting supermarket. If they don't stock them, write to your MP or engage in civil disobedience.

"There is nothing fairer on earth than the sight of a freshly defrosted fish finger."
- Adam Morley, unreconstructed male

Fish may taste great but they are a ludicrous shape. All that tail and fins business means you can't fit one in a lunchbox or a sandwich. It took a British genius to recognise this and so the magnificent fish finger was born. It is an ode to order, a paean to pragmatism, it is brilliance in breadcrumbs.

SERVING SUGGESTION

Align the fingers perpendicular to the edge of the table in front of you. This is not a suggestion. Anything else would be disrespectful to the spirit of the fish finger.

SEWAGE SAYS: **A BIG THUMBS UP**

|Chow Mein| Chow down at your peril

INGREDIENTS

- Noodles
- Chicken, perhaps
- Soy sauce, if you must

FOREIGNNESS

As foreign as dwarf-throwing at the Guardian office party.

People have been eating noodles for over 4,000 years. Which is not surprising because it's almost impossible to wrap them round your fork. And don't even think about using chop sticks. It's like trying to pick up a fresh turd with a piece of string.

THINGS TO WATCH OUT FOR

Finishing your meal then immediately wanting never to eat such a thing again.

SEWAGE SAYS: **SAY NO TO NOODLES**

|Chicken Pie| It's chicken in a pie

INGREDIENTS

- Chicken (free range, if you feel the need)
- Pastry

PREPARATION

Cook the same as veal pie substituting chicken for the veal. The pie bit stays the same.

Chicken pie is a national treasure, the Clare Balding of meat-filled baked pastry. It is food for the people, of the people, by the people. It is not chicken en croute or chicken à la pie. It is, gloriously, unaffectedly... a pie... with chicken in it.

SERVING SUGGESTION

Eat while bemoaning the number of people who are descended from foreigners on *Who Do You Think You Are?*

EWAGE SAYS: **THIS CHICKEN'S GOT WINGS**

How to deny man-made climate change while cooking: #3

Bake a lovely loaf of bread using flour, butter, salt and yeast. The yeast will release carbon dioxide into the rising bread and the atmosphere. Repeat this process for a week. Pop to your allotment to see if your tomato crop has failed. No? That's because man-made climate change is balderdash.

PROPERLY PATRIOTIC
PUDDINGS

EU'll get your just desserts

|Crème Brûlée| French farce

INGREDIENTS

- Cream (burned)
- Sugar (burned)

FOREIGNNESS

As foreign as
a vegetarian in an
all-you-can-eat zoo

Let us unmask this fancy Dan of a dessert for what it really is: a splodge of burned cream. No, sorry. Sometimes there's some burned sugar on top too. Yes, the French have elevated their inability to cook into a national dish. Not only that but crème brûlée contravenes the great rule of British dining: never ever eat anything that contains an accent.

THINGS TO WATCH OUT FOR

A dish so small that neither your spoon nor your tongue will fit inside it. You look at it helplessly for a moment before taking it home and feeding it to your dog.

SEWAGE SAYS: **A CRIME AGAINST COOKIN**

|Custard| A just dessert

INGREDIENTS

- The sap of the custard tree
- Vanilla flavouring

PREPARATION

Whisk then put in a saucepan and cook on a low heat while marvelling at the yellowness of it all.

"The skin on freshly congealed custard is simply unforgettable."
- David Laurence, commendably unfussy eater

Custard is the foot soldier of the sweet course. Unglamorous but gets the job done. You can eat it on its own, pour it on something or hide things in it. It is neither liquid nor solid, neither too sweet nor too bland - a quivering, luscious lump of magnificent British ingenuity.

SERVING SUGGESTION

Can be eaten on its own or with friends who share your views on gay marriage.

EWAGE SAYS: **A TRUE WORKING CLASS HERO**

|Tiramisu| An utter mess

INGREDIENTS

- Coffee (seriously)
- Wine (no, really)
- Cream (we think)

FOREIGNNESS

As foreign as a complimentary glass of champagr on a Ryan Air flight

VETOED

Along with over-sized pepper grinders and over-familiar staff, every restaurant seems to be blighted by this ghastly offering. Just take a look at the ingredients – espresso and wine! Can you believe it? The only time your dessert should contain coffee and wine is when you've had a bloody good evening and knocked your drinks over.

THINGS TO WATCH OUT FOR

Suddenly having the urge to wear your sunglasses at night and shout "ciao bella" while driving a moped really badly.

SEWAGE SAYS: WE WON'T MISS YOU

|Spotted Dick| Down-to-earth pudding

INGREDIENTS

- Suet, flour, raisins cinnamon and stuff like that.

PREPARATION

Mix ingredients and steam for 90 minutes while constantly sniggering to yourself.

A proper dessert with straight-down-the-line ingredients like sponge and currants. What's more, it upholds the great British tradition of harmless sexual innuendo, giving pleasure to customers in restaurants everywhere: "How large will my Spotted Dick be?", and "I'm going to place my Spotted Dick on the table and take a photo". Quality.

SERVING SUGGESTION

Best eaten while watching one of the greatest films ever made: Carry On Dick.

SEWAGE SAYS: **SPOT ON**

|Pavlova| What a palaver

INGREDIENTS

- Caster sugar
- Corn flour
- Don't bother. It gets worse

FOREIGNNESS

As foreign as a skiing instructor who doesn't try to seduce your wife.

Pavlova is proof that you can create evil from anything, even meringue and fruit. Just look at it. It manages to be pompous, vain and inedible all at the same time. Pavlova was apparently created in honour of a Russian dancer touring the Antipodes in the 1920s. What the hell did she do? Defecate on the Australian flag?

THINGS TO WATCH OUT FOR

Suffering ten years' worth of tooth decay in five minutes.

SEWAGE SAYS: **LIKE EATING A FROZEN TEA CO**

|Semolina| Proper school dessert

INGREDIENTS

- Semolina and milk

- Maybe a splodge of jam

PREPARATION

Mix the semolina and milk together until it looks like watery porridge.

"It's impossible to think about semolina pudding without crying."
- **Lucy Mayo, former child**

Other nations consider desserts to be fun, frivolous or even something to look forward to. Not so in Britain. We think a dessert should be character-building. When it's placed in front of you, you feel fear and respect. Life isn't a bowl of cherries, life is a bowl of congealed semolina pudding.

SERVING SUGGESTION

Best given to a young child while telling them the EU Single Market will rob them of their future and that Father Christmas doesn't exist.

NAGE SAYS: **WILL SCAR YOU - IN A GOOD WAY**

How to deny man-made climate change while cooking: #4

Turn your fan-assisted oven up to maximum, use your microwave on full blast and keep all unused electrical appliances on standby. Pop to the pub for a lunchtime ale. Did you spot a drowned polar bear on your journey? No? That's because melting ice-caps is twaddle.

BULLISHLY BRITISH
BEVERAGES

Liquid gumption in a glass

Wine | Fruit juice ruined

INGREDIENTS

- Mouldy grape skin
- Foot sweat

FOREIGNNESS

As foreign as a leaflet shoved through your door you actually want to read.

Is there anything more unBritish than a wine-drinker? Just listen to the tripe they come out with. "I'm getting a hint of cinnamon here, a flirtation of pomegranate, a come-hither wink of something or other." Balderdash. I'll tell you what you get if you drink wine: the sneer of an expensively subsidised ungrateful peasant.

THINGS TO WATCH OUT FOR

Mistaking the wine list for a ransom note.

SEWAGE SAYS: **A WASTE OF GRAPES**

|Gin & Tonic| What a tonic

INGREDIENTS

- Gin
- Tonic
- Ice
- Lemon
- Class

PREPARATION

Throw your wife the car keys and pour yourself a large one.

This was the preferred tipple of the men who ran the Empire. The tonic protected against malaria and the gin protected against sobriety. And it's still a winning combination of health and happiness today. The Queen Mother drank it on her 100th birthday as she asked her daughter: "Where's my bloody telegram then?" God rest her soul and God bless gin and tonic.

SERVING SUGGESTION

Sup on this while explaining the rules of cricket to someone from the Australian cricket team.

SEWAGE SAYS: **TG FOR G&T**

|Latte| Scourge of the high street

INGREDIENTS

- Far too much milk
- Some coffee, so they claim
- Nothing that warrants the price

FOREIGNNESS

As foreign as a snooker table in a caravan.

Skinny latte, soy latte, frappe latte, vanilla latte: there are more varieties than there are ways to enter Britain illegally. It is modern life gone frothing mad. Not only that, it requires a ludicrously complex machine to make it - usually operated by someone doing "training". You want a drink, not an insight into how crap someone can be on their first day at work.

THINGS TO WATCH OUT FOR

Comes in a top-heavy glass that teeters on its tiny saucer, accompanied by a stupidly long spoon that serves no purpose other than to poke you in the eye when drinking.

SEWAGE SAYS: **A GLASS OF HOT MILK RUINE**

|Tea| A pukka cuppa

INGREDIENTS

- Tea leaves
- Hot water
- Milk and sugar

PREPARATION

Being able to make a decent brew is a standard test for mental competence. By that criterion, the rest of the world is barking mad.

"There's nothing that tea can't solve. World peace, quadratic equations, you name it, tea solves it." - **Dominique Harris, woman of great sense**

Like democracy, we might not have invented it but, by God, have we made it our own. Just take the noble British brickie. His veins don't run with blood, they run with "milk and five sugars". Take tea and Page 3 away from him, and he's practically Eastern European. Basically, if you don't test positive for tea then you're not one of us.

SERVING SUGGESTION

English breakfast tea is like a traditional English breakfast, so damned fine that you can have it at any time of the day.

SEWAGE SAYS: **THE KING OF HOT DRINKS**

|Lager| Produces continental hangovers

INGREDIENTS

- Bottom-fermenting yeast
- Too much fizz
- Not enough class

FOREIGNNESS

As foreign as a drum 'n' bass DJ at a funeral

Lager is a comically bland substance made by faceless "beerocrats" in Europe. During the production process any semblance of taste and originality is identified, then carefully removed. Just like they do with their God damn awful so-called "pop" music.

THINGS TO WATCH OUT FOR

Consoling yourself with the thought that your hangover was reassuringly expensive.

SEWAGE SAYS: **URINAL TAP**

|Real Ale| The real deal

INGREDIENTS

- Top-fermenting yeast
- Malted barley and hops

PREPARATION

Go to your local and if they can't offer a pint of Old Fudger's Cockstrap, call the police.

"Just like a British summer's day: dark, cloudy and below room temperature"
- Patrick Green, hard-working beer taster

When Britain ruled the world, a worker would drink pints of ale at lunch before going back to the factory. The result? The Jaguar E-type and Concorde. We built them with a smile on our face. Because we were pissed. Forget what the Nanny State tells you: you must drink this stuff before operating heavy machinery.

SERVING SUGGESTION

Quaff in a thatched inn by a village green as you reflect on the fact that a pint is vastly superior to 0.568 litres.

SEWAGE SAYS: A PINT WELL MADE

Acknowledgements

We give hearty thanks to:

Aaron Budhram, Adam Morley, Alan Dow,

Alan Fox, Alex Fife, Alex Phillips, Angela Fox,

Bake Me, Chris Orrow, Daniel Gosling,

David Laurence, Debbie Sawyer, Dominique Harris,

Elżbieta Marach-Dunajko, Emily Green, Field's,

Fiona Underhill, Gareth Warmingham, Helen Orton,

James Worger, Jane Pepe, John Gowers,

Katie Duncombe, Leon Mayo, libdemvoice.org,

Louisa Gummer, Mary Reid, Miranda Thomas,

Patrick Xavier Green, Paul Sawyer, Reiko Oishi Laurence,

Ric Wegener, Seán Harte, Simon Barker,

Stephen Pepper, Steve Kirkpatrick, Sylvia Odolant,

Tom Pride, UKIP Weather and Yvonne Mowberry.